SandCastle

Word Families Set 8

-ate as in skate

Carey Molter

Consulting Editor Monica Marx, M.A./Reading Specialist

ABDO
Publishing Company

Published by SandCastle™, an imprint of ABDO Publishing Company, 4940 Viking Drive, Edina, Minnesota 55435.

Printed in the United States.

Credits
Edited by: Pam Price
Curriculum Coordinator: Nancy Tuminelly
Cover and Interior Design and Production: Mighty Media
Photo Credits: Eyewire Images, Hemera, Donna Day/ImageState, PhotoDisc

Library of Congress Cataloging-in-Publication Data

Molter, Carey, 1973-
   -Ate as in skate / Carey Molter.
      p. cm. -- (Word families. Set VIII)
      Summary: Introduces, in brief text and illustrations, the use of the letter combination "ate" in such words as "skate," "date," "plate," and "gate."
      ISBN 1-59197-271-X
      1. Readers (Primary) [1. Vocabulary. 2. Reading.] I. Title. II. Series.

PE1119 .M585 2003
428.1--dc21   2002038208

SandCastle™ books are created by a professional team of educators, reading specialists, and content developers around five essential components that include phonemic awareness, phonics, vocabulary, text comprehension, and fluency. All books are written, reviewed, and leveled for guided reading, early intervention reading, and Accelerated Reader® programs and designed for use in shared, guided, and independent reading and writing activities to support a balanced approach to literacy instruction.

Let Us Know

After reading the book, SandCastle would like you to tell us your stories about reading. What is your favorite page? Was there something hard that you needed help with? Share the ups and downs of learning to read. We want to hear from you! To get posted on the ABDO Publishing Company Web site, send us e-mail at:

sandcastle@abdopub.com

SandCastle Level: Beginning

-ate Words

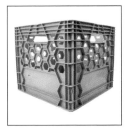

crate

gate

grate

plate

skate

slate

Al unloads the crate.

Todd walks through the gate.

Abe will grate the cheese.

Don holds out his plate.

Amy likes to skate.

There are four words on the slate.

Kate and Nate

There is a frog named Kate.

Kate does push-ups
on her plate.

The plate
is by the skate.

The skate
is in the crate.

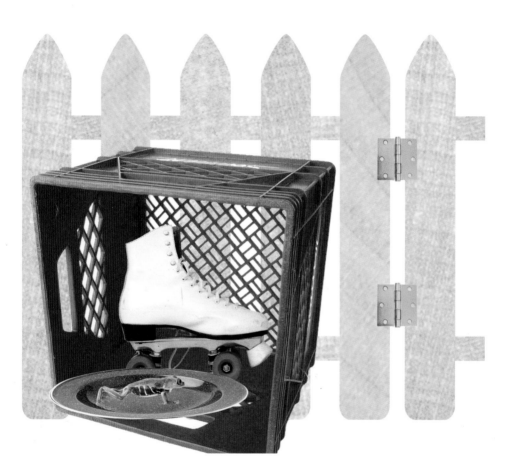

The crate
is by the gate.

Kate looks at
her slate.

She has a date!

She cannot be late!

Kate was not late.

She sees
her pal Nate.

Kate and Nate
went on their date.

They ate and ate
until it was late!

The -ate Word Family

ate	late
crate	mate
date	Nate
fate	plate
gate	rate
grate	skate
hate	slate
Kate	state

Glossary

Some of the words in this list may have more than one meaning. The meaning listed here reflects the way the word is used in the book.

crate   a large box, usually made of wood

date   an appointment to do something with someone else

grate   a framework of metal bars used to cover an opening

slate   a writing tablet that got its name from the gray stone it used to be made of

About SandCastle™

A professional team of educators, reading specialists, and content developers created the SandCastle™ series to support young readers as they develop reading skills and strategies and increase their general knowledge. The SandCastle™ series has four levels that correspond to early literacy development in young children. The levels are provided to help teachers and parents select the appropriate books for young readers.

Emerging Readers
(no flags)

Beginning Readers
(1 flag)

Transitional Readers
(2 flags)

Fluent Readers
(3 flags)

These levels are meant only as a guide. All levels are subject to change.

To see a complete list of SandCastle™ books and other nonfiction titles from ABDO Publishing Company, visit www.abdopub.com or contact us at:

4940 Viking Drive, Edina, Minnesota 55435 • 1-800-800-1312 • fax: 1-952-831-1632